PET PIGS

Advice on management, training and health care

KV-602-050

by

John Walton, PhD, BVM&S, Dip. Bact., DPM, MRCVS

John Carr, PhD, BVSC, Cert.PM, MRCVS

Oliver Duran, DVM, MRCVS

With a Foreword by Lord Runcie of Cuddesdon

and a Preface by Nicholas Soames MP

Illustrations by Jean Wheeler

LIVERPOOL UNIVERSITY PRESS

First published 1992 by
LIVERPOOL UNIVERSITY PRESS
PO Box 147
Liverpool
L69 3BX

British Library Cataloguing in Publication Data
A British Library CIP Record is available

ISBN 0 85323 258 X

Printed by Eaton Press Limited,
Wallasey, Merseyside

FOREWORD

This is an excellent, timely and fascinating handbook. It should be compulsory reading for anyone who keeps a pig as a pet; but it will also appeal to anyone who cares about the welfare of pigs.

Cobbett, in his *Rural Rides*, has a charming little observation. He sees a pig leave a litter, trot on to a little hummock and sniff the direction of the wind. He returns to sow and litter and scuffles up dried leaves to protect them on the appropriate side. Those who know the intelligence and sensitivity of the pig will not be surprised at this story. Yet we don't always realise that we need to display comparable intelligence and sensitivity if our pigs are to be spared needless stress or suffering.

Here is the best specialist advice delivered with an attractive clarity and common sense from which we all can profit.

Lord Runcie of Cuddesdon

CONTENTS

PREFACE

Everyone who keeps animals has a duty to ensure that they are kept in the best possible conditions. No-one should undertake lightly the care of an animal and specialist advice, such as that contained in this booklet, is always to be welcomed.

The pig is an unusual pet. Anyone considering keeping one must understand its special requirements and must pay particular attention to its health and welfare needs. The Ministry's Welfare Code for pigs and welfare legislation are intended for pigs kept on farms, but also contain useful guidance for those who decide to keep pigs as pets. The Ministry's veterinary staff will always provide information on the relevant legal requirements including measures for preventing the spread of diseases, with which every pig keeper has to comply.

The Honourable Nicholas Soames MP
Parliamentary Secretary
Ministry of Agriculture, Fisheries and Food

ACKNOWLEDGEMENTS

The authors are grateful to Mr Peter Attfield and Mrs Jan Davey of Foxes Farm, Ledsham and to Mr and Mrs Geoff Rafferty of The Lodge, Barnston for allowing us to work with their Vietnamese Pot Bellied pets. To Miss Zoe Lindop for introducing us to KuneKune pigs. A special thanks to Mr John Walker, the Divisional Veterinary Officer at Crewe, for his advice on the various legal responsibilities, and to staff at the Animal Welfare Division of the Ministry of Agriculture, Fisheries and Food for their very helpful comments.

INTRODUCTION

The pig is becoming very popular both as an indoor and outdoor pet. Many people treat their pet pigs as they would dogs and cats and, whilst this 'Tender Loving Care' is very commendable, unfortunately it can sometimes present problems for the pig itself. This booklet attempts to set out the 'do's' and 'dont's' for owners of pet pigs in the hope that they will be more understanding of the needs and requirements of their new and exciting pets.

History

The VIETNAMESE POT BELLIED PIG is to be found naturally in the forests of South East Asia, especially around Vietnam. The natives of the region have domesticated what they call the Chinese House Pig, but because of the use of toxic defoliants in the area, not many of these pigs are now to be found in Vietnam. The Pot Bellied Pig came to the UK through Sweden and Canada and is now making inroads into North America.

The KUNEKUNE PIG is thought to have been brought to New Zealand either by the Maoris or by early Chinese settlers. Very few of these pigs are to be found in New Zealand, but attempts are now being made to increase their numbers and recently a small number have been imported into the United Kingdom. As they have always lived in contact with humans, these pigs have developed a very pleasant temperament and will make excellent pets.

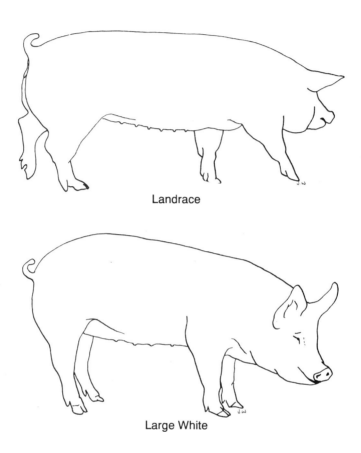

Landrace

Large White

British Saddleback

1. BUYING YOUR PET PIG: POINTS TO CONSIDER

Do not buy a pet pig until you have some basic understanding about the needs of pigs or you have obtained specialist advice from a pig farmer, a vet or another pet pig owner.

Remember that if you want to move your pig away from its home you must obtain a licence from your local Divisional Veterinary Officer. This is an absolute legal requirement and must not be overlooked as failure to do so could be very expensive.

Little newly born piglets are very appealing, but some of the UK domestic breeds of pig grow very big very quickly and can reach over 100kg body weight at 4 months of age.

Pigs can be very destructive to gardens, lawns, fencing, trees, plants, household furniture and fittings.

Pigs have a characteristic odour which will cling to your carpets, clothes and furniture.

Before you buy your pig, always have a well organised pen or some other place ready to put it in and a space for it to exercise so that right from the start it recognises this place as its own. If the pen is indoors make sure the temperature of the room is not less than 18°C.

Finally, when walking your pet pig you must always keep it on a lead and remember to take a big 'pooper scooper' with you. Owning a pet pig must be taken very seriously. Looking after such a pet for 365 days of the year is a very big responsibility, but on the positive side the pig is a very intelligent animal and can give you lots of companionship and plenty of fun.

Types of pig to buy as pets

Basic rules: Commercial breeds such as Landrace, Large White or British Saddleback grow very big, even over 200kg, in a very short time. These are very large pigs and, whilst they can be trained, are not the best household pets because of their size.

Imported breeds of pig: Currently the most popular breed is the Vietnamese Pot Bellied pig, which can live for 15-20 years and will weigh over 65kg when almost fully grown at 18 months old.

The adult Pot Bellied is about 1/4 to 1/2 the size of a commercial pig, it is very round and tubby, usually good tempered, but some individuals can be grumpy and even thoroughly bad tempered. The temperament of any pig is not always obvious in advance of you buying it—because like a dog general demeanour and behaviour depend very much upon how the owner treats, and actually behaves towards, the pig. A very quiet, gentle owner will generally produce a very quiet, gentle pig, whereas a 'bully', or temperamental owner, will often produce a very unpopular pet. Having said this, a few strains of pig are born bad tempered and whatever you do you will not change them.

KuneKune Pigs are small short pigs. They do not get fat and some of them have an upturned nose and mouth. They are well adapted to grazing, but will also live indoors. Their skin is very hairy with a pair of tassles on the throat. Colours range from black to marbled and cream.

2. TRAINING

Almost all pigs can be trained. They respond very well to the reward system of training whereby food or tit bits are offered to attract attention or reward them for something they have done well. Of particular importance is your voice and touch. Pitch and tone of the human voice (without shouting) become very important aids to memory reinforcement for all types of pet and the pig is no exception. The key factors in training are (1) habit, which means repeating the same action over and over again until it is imprinted in your pet's memory; and (2) regular routines, which means that when asking your pet pig to perform a task, give commands in the same manner each time. Always make sure that what you are asking your pig to do is very obvious and not too difficult.

Toilet training for pet pigs that are housed indoors

Take your pet pig outside first thing in the morning and then again at intervals throughout the day. Also remember to use the reward system when your pig performs. Standing your pet on dry litter or newspaper, both of which are very absorbent materials, immediately on waking up and at regular intervals especially after feeding will greatly help in toilet training. If your pet pig is to be kept in a pen make sure that the floor space is divided into two areas to keep the straw bedding in the sleeping area and the other part free of bedding for exercise and toilet activities.

Introducing your new pig to established pets within the house

When introducing your new pet pig into a household that already has an established dog or cat, make the introduction gradually and very soon your 'old' pet will accept the new member of the household and may even develop a strong and lasting relationship with it. A word of warning - be very careful when introducing and mixing a new pig with one already present in the house or garden. Usually the two of them will fight very seriously, so it is best to keep them apart until they know each other well.

3. HOUSING

The most important point to remember when deciding on the type of housing to use is that pigs cannot sweat, so they must be provided with conditions that allow them to stay cool, especially during the hot summer months. This can be done by providing them with a shallow pool of clean water in which to wallow and some form of cover to provide shade from the sun. Pigs in hot sun can suffer very badly from sunstroke, and both black and white skinned pigs can develop very bad sunburn. Some owners like their pets to wallow in mud, which when dried on the skin can provide some protection from the sun.

Take special care before putting pigs outdoors to make sure that there is a very strong wire fence around all the area in which the pig is going to exercise or else you will have serious disputes with your neighbours after their garden has been rooted up.

The best type of pen is one that is divided into two parts by a thick piece of wood bolted to the floor. This will keep the straw bedding in place at one end and a non-bedded toilet and exercise area at the other end. This arrangement also provides a rough concrete surface to keep the feet in trim, which also helps to prevent the toes from overgrowing. If your pet is to be housed indoors then do not expect it to sleep on a cold bare floor—this must be covered with clean dry straw or a rug to provide comfort both for legs and joints and insulation against the cold.

One very important point to remember when housing your pet pig indoors is that, because of its very inquisitive nature, electrical cables to television sets and table lamps will very soon be chewed through. So always keep electric cables out of reach and hidden behind wooden or plastic trunking. Young piglets are very playful and will readily accept toys to play with. Make sure these are very strong and are not easily broken into small pieces that can be swallowed and cause stomach problems.

Owners should refer to the *Code of Recommendations for the Welfare of Livestock:Pigs*, which has a section devoted to housing.

4. FEEDING

Whilst pigs are omnivorous (this means they can eat almost anything), they do best if kept on a barley-based ration to which you can add fruits, vegetables, fish or milk. Do not give your pet pig just one meal a day. The best routine is to give it food little and often, especially for indoor pets. Do not be tempted to overfeed or give too much protein in the diet, as females in particular will put on too much weight and this may produce breeding problems later on. Always remember that your pig must have fresh water available at all times, otherwise it could develop salt poisoning from water deprivation. With outdoor pets the routine will be different because all pigs like to root in the earth for all kinds of goodies. But even so outdoor pigs will need a ration of concentrated feed that you can buy from the corn merchant or your local pig farmer. Give this once a day if pigs are allowed prolonged grazing, and twice a day if they are not allowed to graze at all. As a general rule never feed more than 1-2% of the pig's body weight in one day. Finally, it is illegal to feed waste food because many serious diseases can be spread to pigs by this means. Your own kitchen scraps could be classed as waste food—see chapter 10 for a precise definition.

5. HANDLING

Dont's

(1) Never pick a piglet up by its ears or tail. This is most painful and will make the piglet very wary of being picked up at all in the future.

(2) Never chase or frighten piglets before picking them up as this will only upset them and can cause severe distress and difficulty in breathing.

Do's

(1) Always pick up a piglet as you would a human baby gather it up with two hands around its body and hold it firmly in your arms or even under one arm—if you don't hold it close to you it will struggle, become very excited and may fall to the floor and hurt itself.

(2) When handling any age of pig always remember to make use of your voice—pigs soon get used to their owner's voice and will respond accordingly.

(3) The best way to get your pig's attention is to offer it some food. A pig will always come for food and then you can pick it up or direct it into a pen or put on its collar and lead.

Remember

A bad tempered owner will nearly always produce a bad tempered or mentally disturbed pig—so make sure you handle your pet with consideration, don't bully it, don't scream at it and don't use physical violence. For the best results always remember to use Tender Loving Care (TLC).

Young lovable piglets eventually grow old, they can develop arthritis, they may not see very well, teeth and feet may grow rather too long and need attention from the vet.

6. EXERCISE

To keep your pet pig fit and healthy you must provide it with regular exercise. Try and aim for 20 minutes exercise twice daily. If left to their own devices pigs will sleep for the greater part of the day, especially if kept indoors or in a pen. In devising an exercise schedule, bear in mind why you want your pet to have exercise.

Some reasons for exercise

(1) To keep the limbs, heart and lungs in good condition.
(2) To provide a natural way of keeping the toe nails from growing too long.
(3) To build up an appetite for food.
(4) To help prevent your pet from getting too fat and bored.
(5) To help avoid constipation.

Exercising

A common way of exercising one or more pigs is to put food either on the floor or in a food trough at some distance from the pen or house door, then let the pig out and call to it to come and eat. The first time you may need to tempt the pig with some food in your hand and at the same time call or whistle. Very soon the pig will get the message and when you call it will come galloping towards you to get its food, but remember don't feed more than the daily allocation including tit-bits (see page 8).

Remember: Exercising must take place on concrete or rough ground as well as on soft sandy ground because good foot care does rely upon the sole of the foot being kept worn down by continual contact with a rough surface. However, you must be careful not to wear down the feet too much, otherwise they will become painful and your pet will become very lame. Also try not to exercise in direct sunlight unless your pet is used to it.

A very good way of exercising both owner and pig is to run ahead of the pig—tempting it initially with food, but stopping this as soon as possible to avoid the pig getting too many tit-bits and probably becoming too fat and overweight.

Collar and lead

The best type of collar is one that encircles the neck and the body just behind the front legs. A broad, soft-leather or canvas band can be used with a lead that is about 10-20 feet long and has a hand loop for safety.

7. REPRODUCTION

Owners should think very seriously before deciding to breed from their pets. More pigs mean more expense, more space requirements, more waste matter to dispose of and, especially, what are you going to do with the extra piglets? Do you want to sell them, keep them or give them away, and have new owners been found beforehand? These matters all require very careful consideration before you start to breed more litters.

Points about breeding (these do not apply to Wild Boar pigs)

(1)   All domestic female pigs can breed about twice every year.

(2)   Breeding females will start their first cycle or heat period (which means that they will accept the boar for mating) at about six months of age and will continue to cycle regularly every 21 days for very many years.

(3)   Boars are ready to begin breeding at about nine months of age, although some will begin to mount females as early as four months.

(4)   It is not always very easy to recognise 'cycling' in individual female pigs that are kept on their own, so a boar is usually needed to highlight the physiological signs of willingness or readiness of the female to be mated. These signs are:

The sow may be more alert, her ears may be 'pricked' (erect), her voice may be pitched higher, she may carry bedding in her mouth, she may squeal, she may go off her food, but especially, very soon after showing signs of heat,   she will stand very firmly and be unwilling to move when her owner leans on her back. This 'standing position' is perhaps the best way of telling when a female pig is ready for mating. Some of the white breeds of pigs may, with their first heat only, show reddening of the vulva (the outside part of the female reproductive organs), which also may be a little swollen and moist.

The period of heat will last for about 24-36 hours—but this will vary depending on the time of year and the nearness of the boar (smell, touch, hearing and sight of the boar will always intensify the signs of heat in the sow).

Mating

If a family of pigs is kept together, then there should be no need for any help by the owner with mating. However, if the male and female are kept apart, then the owner may have to give some assistance. If a boar is available, then the sow should be mated twice, with a 24-hour interval between matings. If a boar is not available and the sow has to be artificially inseminated, then semen must be ordered at the first sign of heat (good record keeping will also help to predict this date) and there must be two inseminations spaced about twelve hours apart, with the first one being made between 12 and 24 hours after the onset of heat, which is as soon as the female adopts the 'standing for service' position. Always make sure that plenty of time is allowed both for natural mating and artificial insemination. Too much of a hurry will inevitably result in a failure to achieve pregnancy. If any problems occur at any stage of the mating process then call your vet.

Owners who don't want their pet sows to become pregnant:

(1)   Have the sow sterilised between 4-6 months of age.
(2)   Have the boar sterilised or vasectomised at about 4-6 months of age.
(3)   Don't keep a boar.
(4)   Some owners prefer to have their pet sows sterilised even though they don't have a boar because when the sow has a heat period she often forgets her toilet training and this will cause problems in the house.

Precautions to take when your pet sow has piglets

When the babies are due, your pet sow will usually make a nest and she will usually be very active for the final 1 or 2 days. Just before delivery begins the sow will settle down by her nest, she may refuse food, but water must always be available. Imminent signs of giving birth include milk in the teats, a relaxed area of skin around and below the tail and, of course, straining. When the piglets are being born the sow's tail will wag as the piglets pass through her pelvis and her uppermost hind leg may be drawn forward during straining. Generally the piglets are born about 15 minutes apart or sometimes there is a rush, with several of them being born almost at once. Because of the small size of the piglets, they can be born front-end or tail-end first and delivery problems very rarely occur; if they do then you must call your vet immediately. Once farrowing has finished, a 'bag-like' after-birth will be passed by the sow and this really indicates that the birth process has ended. Apart from checking that all the baby piglets are breathing well, have been rubbed dry with a towel and are sucking, nothing further needs doing to them as the sow will now take care of all their needs. One word of caution: sows with newly born litters can be very protective and will defend them very vigorously—so take care—disturb mother and piglets as little as possible. Once the novelty has passed, many sows will allow their piglets to be picked up and handled, but always be on your guard. Once the piglets have been born they need to be put into an area next to the sow where the air temperature is not less than 29°C. This temperature must be kept for at least 7 days, after which it can gradually be reduced to normal room temperature of 21°C.

Feeding the sow during suckling

The sow needs to eat her normal amount of food plus some more for milk production. This extra amount needs to be equal to about half the weight of the litter in kg of food (if the total weight of the litter is 5 kg, then the sow should receive her normal maintenance ration plus 2.5kg more to provide milk for the piglets). This extra amount needs to be given gradually over 7-10 days as the sow's appetite increases. This increased amount of food must be continued until weaning when it can be reduced quite quickly back to the maintenance level. Don't forget that a lactating sow always needs fresh drinking water to be available.

Weaning

This will take place at about 4-5 weeks of age, although some people like the piglets to wean themselves. You must be careful that the sow does not lose too much weight or too much calcium during a prolonged lactation period. When the piglets are eating solid food and mum's milk supply is decreasing, then the piglets can be removed, weaned and housed on their own.

Feeding piglets after weaning

A high protein diet will only be needed if the piglets are weaned at three weeks of age, but if they are left on the sow for a longer period then normal food will be adequate. The high protein weaner diet can be purchased from the corn merchant or your local pig farmer.

8. HEALTH PROBLEMS

During its lifetime your pig may need the attention of a veterinary surgeon, especially if you have never looked after pigs before. Failure to get professional help when your pet is off-colour could well delay its recovery and may even be life-threatening. It is advisable, therefore, to check that the local veterinary surgery, particularly if located in an urban area, has 'in-house' expertise in dealing with pigs.

(1)   *Flakey skin* - Always be on the watch for infestation by mange mites, which   will cause your pet to be very itchy and have a yellowish-brown deposit on the skin, particularly in and around the ears. Lice, if present, may be difficult to see on a dark-skinned pig, but they are about 0.5cm long, dark-coloured and move very fast on the hairy parts of the pig's skin. Your vet will be able to give you something to get rid of them. Flakey skin is also due to the skin becoming very dry and can be cured by rubbing in baby oil or emulsifying soap. Occasional bathing can be great fun for your pet—use lukewarm water and a very mild shampoo. Remember to put a mat on the bottom of a low-sided bath to prevent your pet slipping and hurting itself and remember you could hurt your back.

(2)   *Sunburn*—This can be a very serious problem with both light- and dark-skinned pigs. It is always better to avoid sunburn by providing shade and also water to wallow in. Overheating of the pig by strong sunlight can lead to sunstroke. Treatment of sunburn involves both cooling the pig with a water spray and coating the pig's back with baby lotion. If the sunburn is very bad, call your vet because special treatment will be required.

(3)   *Running eyes*—This condition may be due to inflammation of the lining of the snout, irritation of the eye with bent or damaged eyelashes; and very often outdoor pigs get soil or sand in the eye, but this can

easily be rinsed out. If, after rinsing the eye with Optrex eye lotion, the condition persists, call your vet.

(4) *Failure to eat* - This can be due to several things, such as: (a) the pig having a high temperature when it will feel hot, especially around its ears and may be breathing rapidly with its mouth open - then you must call your vet; (b) the pig doesn't like the food that is offered; (c) the pig has already eaten too much; and (d) sufficient water is not available.

(5) *Insect bites*—During the summer there are lots of biting flies and other insects about, and if they attack and bite your pig they will cause tender raised lumps to appear on its skin. Washing the pig with a mild antiseptic solution will help to prevent the bites becoming infected.

(6) *Water deprivation*—If your pig is deprived of water for any length of time it will begin to wander about aimlessly, and it may start to stagger and bump into things. Its voice will become high-pitched and it may seem to be blind. This is because salt has built up in the pig's body and has not been got rid of by the natural process of drinking and urinating. The condition is called 'salt poisoning'. Treatment consists of pouring water gently over the side of the mouth when the pig will start to lap it up. Continue giving water in this manner, little and often, until your pet is able to stand and drink for itself. Never pour water into the pig's mouth as this may cause water to enter the lungs, which is very dangerous and could cause pneumonia. The best advice is not to let water deprivation occur by always keeping fresh water available.

(7) Feet—overgrown toes will need trimming by your vet.

(8) Joints—arthritis is not uncommon in older pigs and is made worse by wet, cold and unbedded concrete floors. Pigs with affected joints should be provided with dry, warm and comfortable bedding. Serious cases of arthritic lameness will require treatment by your vet.

9. DISEASE PREVENTION

Some diseases can be prevented by regular vaccination together with routine annual or six-monthly boosters. These diseases include:

(1) *Erysipelas (measles)*: An initial course of two injections, followed by a six-monthly booster will totally prevent the appearance of this disease. Vaccination against this disease is a must for all piggy pets, especially those kept outdoors.

(2) *Parvovirus infection:* This causes very small litters to be born, together with several mummified piglets. Again, the disease can be totally prevented by regular vaccination.

Other pig vaccines are available to prevent such diseases as piglet enteritis, but this disease is generally only seen with very large groups of piglets and failure of management to provide individual piglet care, or when the air temperature and humidity fluctuate too widely for the newly-born piglets.

Diarrhoea (Scours)

This commonly occurs with overfeeding, especially just after weaning time and also if the piglets are weaned too early. As a rule of thumb, it is better to allow piglets to continue to suck their mums for 4-6 weeks, whilst at the same time eating the same food as the sow, who will encourage the piglets to eat whilst she is eating. If diarrhoea is present in all piglets in the litter, then you need to call your vet for advice because there are also infectious causes of diarrhoea which may require antibiotic therapy.

Worming

Pigs that live outdoors and pigs that are exercised outside need to be dosed for worms every 4-6 months. The decision when to dose can be helped by taking a dung sample to the vet, who will examine it for worm eggs and decide which is the best treatment to use and when to use it.

Pneumonia

This infection of the lungs will occur usually in housed pigs when they are subjected to cold draughts or rapid changes in environmental temperature and if the pigs are allowed to sleep on damp, wet or cold floors. The pig will have a high temperature and you will need to call your vet to give it some antibiotics.

10. LEGAL REQUIREMENTS

The Pig and the Law

The domestic pig is farmed in the UK to provide meat for human consumption. There is widespread national and international trade in live pigs, pig meat and boar semen. In order to prevent the spread of disease from other countries to UK pigs, a variety of laws and regulations have been introduced by the Government over the years and these apply to all types of pigs, whether kept in the house as a pet or on the farm.

(1)   *Scraps of waste human food:* These must **never** be fed to pet pigs. Waste food is defined by law as any meat, bones, blood, offal or other part of the carcase of any livestock or of any poultry, or product derived therefrom or hatchery waste or eggs or egg shells. Also any broken or waste foodstuffs (including table or kitchen refuse, scraps or waste) which contain or have been in contact with meat, bones, blood, offal or with any other part of the carcase of any livestock or of any poultry. It does not include pig meal manufactured from protein originating from livestock or poultry. Great care must be taken in this matter, for example bread from a meat sandwich must not be given to pigs because it has been in contact with meat, which is a prohibited food.

(2)   *Buying and selling and moving pigs:* In order to move a pig from one place to another the owner must get a certificate from the local Ministry of Agriculture, Fisheries and Food Divisional Veterinary Officer (DVO). The address of this official can be obtained from your own veterinary surgeon. To get a certificate to exercise your pet you must: (a) specify a route that you will be using; (b) keep your pet on a lead at all times when exercising or moving it; (c) there must be no contact with any other pig; (d) your pet must not have been fed any waste food at any time; and (e) **you must not exercise your pet on agricultural land**. A certificate, when authorised, will last 12 months, after which it must be renewed. A condition of the

certificate is that the owner must carry it whilst the pet is being exercised and produce it on demand to a police constable, inspector or other officer of the Ministry of Agriculture. The certificate carries a list of prohibited waste foods, which as indicated above must **never** be fed to pet pigs.

Taking your pig to a pet show: If you want to take your pig to a pet show, then a licence has to be obtained from your local authority (Trading Standards Office). This licence authorises the movement of your pet to a named show and its subsequent return to your home premises, and the same conditions will be applied as for an exercise certificate. It is a condition of the licence that on return home your pet must be kept separate from other pigs for a period of 21 days. If during this 21-day period the pig is to be exhibited at another show or exhibition then a request will have to be made to the Trading Standards Officer.

Transport: When moving your pig always use a trailer that has been thoroughly washed and disinfected, followed by rinsing out with clean water, to prevent irritation of the skin, before and after movement with a disinfectant approved for Swine Vesicular Disease. These approved disinfectants can be purchased either from your local pet shop or agricultural merchant's store. Note that iodine-based disinfectants may cause an allergic skin reaction on your pig.

(3)   *Treating health problems in pets:* As the owner of a pet pig you can treat it with a variety of medicines, some of which may be obtained at the local pet shop; others, like antibiotics, can only be obtained on prescription from a veterinary surgeon. If you need to visit the vet's surgery with your pig, because it has a health problem, then you are permitted to do this, but you must notify your local DVO immediately afterwards. **In the event of an emergency** your pig should not be taken to the vet —you must call the vet to come and see it.

11. PIG LORE

Many sayings about pigs reflect more of the habits and deficiencies of their owners than the natural behaviour of the pig.

For instance, 'happy as a pig in muck' is a saying that seems to indicate that pigs are dirty animals and love to lie in dirty conditions. There is nothing further from the truth—allow a pig to develop good habits and provide it with a clean, dry bedded area and you will soon see one of the cleanest animals imaginable. Pigs will only lie in dirty conditions if there is nowhere else to go, such as when the owner does not clean out the pen, or if the pen is too small for the pig to have separate sleeping and dunging areas. It is very important to clean out pens on a daily basis because in hot weather the pigs will lie down in the faeces and urine to keep cool.

Another saying goes 'a fat pig is a happy pig'. Very fat pigs are not happy—they have difficulty walking, they may even have great difficulty mating and they certainly cannot keep cool in hot weather. Allowing a pig to get too fat, in fact allowing any pet to get too fat, is a very cruel practice indeed and must not be allowed to happen because it prevents your pet from doing all those things that it likes to do.

'Pig sick' is also very misleading. Pigs are very healthy animals indeed and generally will only become sick if the owner does not look after them properly.

12. PIGGY FACTS AND FABLES

* St Anthony is the patron saint of swine herds.

* Pigs are still used in France to find truffles in the ground.

* Pigs, because of their very discriminating sense of smell, are being used by some international police forces to detect smuggled drugs and narcotics.

* In some American states pig racing is a very popular sport.

* The heaviest recorded pig weighed over 1158kg.

* Pigs cannot perspire—they lose heat by open-mouth panting—hence the need to provide them with some shade in hot sunny weather.

* Pig's Snout is the name of a variety of apple.

* Pig's Nose is the name of a blend of Scotch Whisky.

13. BASIC HEALTH INFORMATION (NOT ALL APPLICABLE TO THE WILD BOAR)

* Normal body temperature (rectal) 39°C (102°F).

* Length of pregnancy 115 ± 2 days.

* Frequency of heat (oestrus) 21 ± 1 day.

* Breeding cycles occur all year round.

* Number of piglets born per litter can be anything from 4-6.

* Pigs are omnivorous, but their usual diet is based on barley.

14. WELFARE REQUIREMENTS

Welfare refers to the quality of life that an animal experiences and can be thought of in terms of the 'five freedoms' that all animals should be expected to enjoy. These are freedom from thirst, hunger and malnutrition, freedom from injury, disease and infestation, freedom to display most natural patterns of behaviour, freedom from fear and the freedom to be provided with appropriate comfort and shelter.

Look after your pet well, understand its basic requirements and always ensure that it has a warm, dry place to sleep and somewhere to exercise. Provide it with good wholesome food to eat and see that fresh clean water is always available for it to drink.

15. SOCIAL AWARENESS

When accepting a pet pig into the family group, there are certain considerations, as with other animals, that you should always keep in mind concerning the disturbance that a pig may cause to your neighbours.

Firstly, you need to take into account the amount of faeces and urine that one pig produces in a year, because cleaning and disposal of these will provide you with a very important problem, especially if you only have a very small garden in a town centre or, worse still, no garden at all. One adult pig will produce about six kilograms of faeces and urine every day, which is over two tonnes in one year. These animal waste products, if not removed promptly, will produce an offensive odour and, due to their high ammonia levels and bacterial content, may be a health risk both to humans and pigs alike. One possible way of dealing with this problem is to mix the pig waste (faeces, urine and soiled straw) with grass, flower cuttings or vegetable waste in a compost heap and allow everything to decompose. Remember that this process can produce a very potent odour to which your neighbours may object very strongly.

Noise is also an important consideration, particularly when several pigs are kept together in a group, and the very loud noise that they can produce will cause tension with your neighbours.

Another factor to be aware of is that, even though most pigs are friendly, their considerable weight and agility can be very hazardous for young children who might want to play with them.

Finally, you must always check that there is no clause in the deeds for your house which prohibits the keeping of pigs, as failure to appreciate this could involve you in expensive litigation matters with your neighbours and landlord.

16. USEFUL ADDRESSES AND FURTHER READING

(1)   The Pig Veterinary Society, c/o The British Veterinary Association, 7 Mansfield Street, London W1M OAT.

(2)   The British Pig Association, 7 Rickmansworth Road, Watford, Hertfordshire, WD1 7HE.

(3)   The Rare Breeds Trust, National Agricultural Centre, Stoneleigh, Warwickshire.

Codes of Recommendations for the Welfare of Livestock: Pigs, Leaflet 702, MAFF Publications, London SE99 7TP.

'Handling Pigs' by John Walton, in *Practical Animal Handling*, Edited by R. S. Anderson and A. T. B. Edney, Pergamon Press, 1991.

INDEX